Structure & Speaking Practice
Hong Kong

NATIONAL GEOGRAPHIC
LEARNING

Australia • Brazil • Mexico • Singapore • United Kingdom • United States

National Geographic Learning,
a Cengage Company

Structure & Speaking Practice, Hong Kong

Nancy Douglas and James R. Morgan

Publisher: Sherrise Roehr

Executive Editor: Laura LeDréan

Managing Editor: Jennifer Monaghan

Digital Implementation Manager,
Irene Boixareu

Senior Media Researcher: Leila Hishmeh

Director of Global Marketing: Ian Martin

Regional Sales and National Account
Manager: Andrew O'Shea

Content Project Manager: Ruth Moore

Senior Designer: Lisa Trager

Manufacturing Planner: Mary Beth
Hennebury

Composition: Lumina Datamatics

Student Edition: Structure & Speaking Practice, Hong Kong
ISBN-13: 978-0-357-13789-5

National Geographic Learning
20 Channel Center Street
Boston, MA 02210
USA

Locate your local office at **international.cengage.com/region**

Visit National Geographic Learning online at **ELTNGL.com**
Visit our corporate website at **www.cengage.com**

Printed in China
Print Number: 01   Print Year: 2019

Photo Credits

SCOPE & SEQUENCE

Unit / Lesson	Video	Vocabulary	Listening

Grammar	Pronunciation	Speaking	Reading	Writing	Communication
* Subject pronouns and possessive adjectives with *be* * Yes / No questions and short answers with *be*	Contractions with *be*	Introducing yourself	Famous name changers Read for details Scan for information	Write about favorites	* Complete forms with personal information; Interview classmates * Ask and answer questions about favorites
* Questions and answers with *who* and *where* * Adjectives with *be*	Stressed syllables	Asking where someone is from	A great place to visit Scan for information Read for details	Describe a favorite place	* Ask and answer questions about places * Choose a vacation spot
* Spelling rules for forming plural nouns * This / that / these / those	Plural endings	Giving and replying to thanks	The one thing I can't live without Infer information Scan for information	Read and describe a product review	* Give and receive gifts * Rate a product Collect data in a chart
* The present continuous tense: affirmative and negative statements * The present continuous tense: extended time	Question intonation	Greeting people and asking how they are	Study abroad Identify main ideas Infer meaning Find key details	Answer interview questions	* Play charades Act out and identify actions * A student interview Interview classmates

Language Summaries p. 66   Grammar Notes p. 69

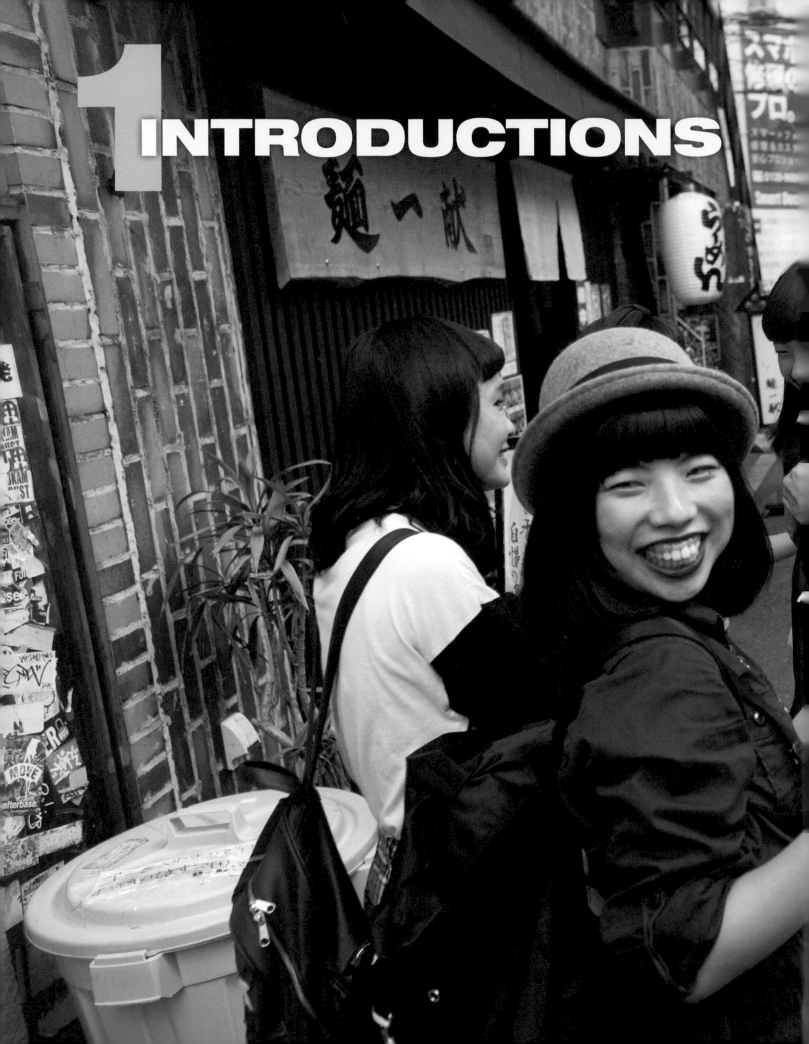

1 INTRODUCTIONS

Look at the photo. Point to the picture and say the sentences. Then answer the question.

1 They are students.

2 They are friends.

3 Her name is Aya.

4 What's your name?

UNIT GOALS

1 Introduce yourself

2 Describe and answer questions about yourself and other people

3 Talk about your favorite TV shows, sports, and music

4 Read and spell email addresses

A group of students in Osaka, Japan

Students say "Hi" outside of school.

1 **VIDEO** Carlos's Day

A ▶ Watch the video. Repeat the sentences aloud as you watch.

B ▶ Watch the video again. This time, some sentences will be blank. Match the correct answers to complete the conversation.

1. _____   a. She's a student.
2. _____   b. See you!
3. _____   c. Hi!
4. _____   d. Bye!
5. _____   e. Hello!
6. _____   f. He's a student.

C 🔁 Now say "Hi" and "Bye" to a partner.

2 VOCABULARY

A Complete the ID cards. Use the class list below.

STUDENT ID
UNIVERSITY
First name: **Yukiko**
Last name: _____
ID number: 488
Male ___
Female **X**

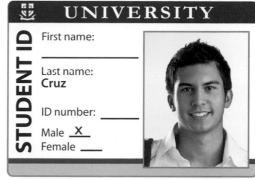

STUDENT ID
UNIVERSITY
First name: _____
Last name: **Cruz**
ID number: _____
Male **X**
Female ___

STUDENT ID
UNIVERSITY
First name: **Carlos**
Last name: _____
ID number: _____
Male **X**
Female ___

STUDENT ID
UNIVERSITY
First name: **Liling**
Last name: _____
ID number: _____
Male ___
Female **X**

Class List: English 101		
Last name	**First name**	**Student ID number**
Akita	Yukiko	488
Cruz	Alberto	307
Ramalho	Carlos	592
Wong	Liling	169

i Numbers 0–10

0 zero	4 four	8 eight
1 one	5 five	9 nine
2 two	6 six	10 ten
3 three	7 seven	

B 🔊 Listen. Check your answers. **Track 1**

C 🔁 Make a student ID card for a partner. Ask him or her these questions.

What's your first name?

What's your last name?

What's your ID number?

3 LISTENING

A Answer the questions with a partner.

1. How do you spell your name?
2. Do you have a nickname (another name) or a short name?
3. What is your email address?

> My last name is Diaz.

> How do you spell that?

> It's spelled D-I-A-Z.

Reading email addresses

@ = "at"
.com = "dot com"
.edu = "dot e-d-u"

Common types of email addresses

(business name) .com
(school name) .edu
(organization name) .org

B **Listen for details**. Listen. Fill in the nicknames. Then fill in Joshua's last name.
Track 2

HELLO

1. My name is ____Joshua____.

   In this class, call me: _____.

HELLO

2. My name is ____Yukiko Akita____.

   In this class, call me: _____.

   Email address: Yukiko@_____

HELLO

3. My name is ____Alberto Cruz____.

   In this class, call me: _____.

   Email address: Alberto@_____

HELLO

4. My name is ____Liling Wong____.

   In this class, call me: _____.

   Email address: Liling@_____

C Listen to the full conversation. Complete the email addresses. **Track 3**

D Say and spell the names and email addresses of each person with a partner.

4 SPEAKING

A 🔊 🔄 **Pronunciation: Contractions with *be*.** Practice saying these full and contracted (shorter) forms with a partner. Then listen and repeat. **Track 4**

I am → I'm → I'm a student.

What is → What's → What's your name?

It is → It's → It's nice to meet you.

B 🔊 **Pronunciation: Contractions with *be*.** Say the words in blue with your instructor. Then listen to the audio. Circle the words you hear. **Track 5**

1. A: Hi, I am / I'm Ken.

   B: What is / What's your last name, Ken?

   A: It is / It's Tanaka.

   B: Great. And what is / what's your student ID number?

   A: It's 524.

2. A: What is / What's your name, please?

   B: It is / It's Maria Fuentes.

   A: Hmmm, you are / you're not on my class list. Your last name is Fuentes?

   B: Yes, that is / that's right.

C 🔄 **Pronunciation: Contractions with *be*.** Practice the dialogs in **B** with a partner.

D 🔊 🔄 Listen to the conversation. Then practice with a partner. **Track 6**

LILING: Hi, my name's Liling. What's your name?

ALBERTO: Hi, Liling. I'm Alberto, but please call me Beto. It's my nickname.

LILING: Okay, Beto. Nice to meet you.

ALBERTO: It's nice to meet you, too.

E 🔄 Practice the conversation again with your partner. Use your own names.

SPEAKING STRATEGY

F 👥 Use the Useful Expressions. Meet six classmates. Write their names in the box.

My classmates

1. _____
2. _____
3. _____
4. _____
5. _____
6. _____

Useful Expressions
Introducing yourself
Hi, what's your name?
Hi, my name is Liling.
I'm Liling. / It's Liling.
My name is Mr. Porter.
I'm Alberto, but please call me Beto.
(It's) nice to meet you.
(It's) nice to meet you, too.
Speaking Tip
You can use *My name is…* or *I'm…* to introduce yourself.

G 🔄 Say your classmates' names to a partner.

5 GRAMMAR

A Turn to page 69. Complete the exercises. Then do **B** and **C** below.

Subject Pronouns with *be*			
Subject pronoun	***be***		**Subject pronoun contractions with *be***
I	**am**		I am = I'm
You	**are**	a student.	you are = you're
He / She	**is**		he is = he's / she is = she's

Possessive Adjectives with *be*			
Possessive adjective		***be***	
My			
Your	last name	**is**	Smith.
His / Her			

B Look at the pictures. Then play the memory game with your class. How far can you go?

1 My name is Rina. I'm a student.

2 Your name is Rina. You are a student. My name is Lucas. I am a student.

3 Your name is Rina. You are a student. Your name is Lucas. You are a student. My name is Jen. I am a student.

C Play again. This time use numbers and *he, his*, *she*, and *her*.

1 My name is Rina. I am a student. My number is 8.

2 Her name is Rina. She is a student. Her number is 8. My name is Lucas. I am a student. My number is 3.

3 Her name is Rina. She is a student. Her number is 8. His name is Lucas. He is a student. His number is 3. My name is Jen....

6 COMMUNICATION

A Look at the answers. Write the correct questions.

1. What's _____?

   My name is Ariana Valdez.

2. _____?

   My email address is avaldez@eazypost.com.

3 _____?

   My phone number is (399) 555-7061.

B Imagine you are a new student. Make up a new name, phone number, and email address. Complete the form.

The English School of Melbourne, Australia

_____   _____
Last name   First name

(613)_____   _____
Phone number   Email address

C 🔗 Meet four students. Write their information below. Use your "new" information from above.

Student 1
Last name: _____
First name: _____
Phone number: _____
Email address: _____

Student 3
Last name: _____
First name: _____
Phone number: _____
Email address: _____

Student 2
Last name: _____
First name: _____
Phone number: _____
Email address: _____

Student 4
Last name: _____
First name: _____
Phone number: _____
Email address: _____

1 VOCABULARY

A 🔁 Look at the boxes. Then think of two other kinds of music and sports. Tell a partner.

B 🔁 Look at Chrissy's web page above. Complete the sentences with a partner.

1. Chrissy **is friends with** _____ people.

2. Her **favorlte sport** is _____.

3. Her favorite **player** is _____.

4. Her favorite kinds of **music** are _____ and _____.

5. Her favorite **TV show** is _____.

6. Her favorite **singers** are _____ and _____.

7. Her favorite **movie** is _____.

8. Her favorite **actor** is Benedict Cumberbatch. Her favorite _____ is Jennifer Lawrence.

Music	
🎻	classical
📻	pop
🎤	rap
🎸	rock
Sports	
⚾	baseball
🏀	basketball
⚽	soccer
🎾	tennis

C 🔁 Talk about your friends and favorite things. Make eight sentences like the ones in **B**. Tell a partner.

My favorite TV show is....

2 LISTENING

A 🔁 Point to a photo. Use one of the sentences below to describe it to a partner. Take turns.

It's a reality show.   It's a scary show.   It's a soccer game.

B 🔊 **Listen for gist.** Listen to a man and woman talk about shows on TV. Number each show (1, 2, or 3) as they talk about it. **Track 7**

C 🔊 **Listen for details.** Listen again. Which show do they watch? Circle it. **Track 7**

D 🔁 Do people watch shows like this in your country? What other shows are popular in your country? Tell a partner.

Soccer is popular.

... is also popular.

3 READING 🔊 Track 8

A 🔄 Look at the people. Do you know their names? Tell a partner.

B 🔄 **Read for details.** Work with a partner.

- **Student A:** Read about people 1 and 2.
  Student B: Read about people 3 and 4.

- Underline each person's nickname or new name. Circle his or her real or full name. For person 1, circle why nobody knows his real name.

C 🔄 **Scan for information.** Talk about one of your two people. Say the person's real or full name, and his or her nickname or new name. Your partner takes notes and asks questions.

> This is Paul Van Haver. He's a singer.

> What's his nickname?

> It's....

> Can you spell that, please?

D 🔄 Read about your partner's person or people. Check your answers in **C**.

FAMOUS NAME CHANGERS

1 BANKSY is a street artist and filmmaker from the United Kingdom. No one knows his real name, and there are no pictures of him. This way he can do his work freely.

2 **GIVANILDO VIEIRA DE SOUSA** is a soccer player from Brazil. His nickname is Hulk. Why? He's very strong, but he also looks like The Hulk!

3 **J. K. ROWLING** is a writer and the author of the *Harry Potter* books. Her full name is Joanne Kathleen Rowling, but her friends call her Jo.

4 **PAUL VAN HAVER** is a famous hip-hop singer from Belgium, but everyone knows him as Stromae. The name *Stromae* comes from changing the sounds in the word *maestro*[1] from *mae – stro* to *stro – mae*.

[1]A *maestro* is a great musician.

4 GRAMMAR

A Turn to page 70. Complete the exercises. Then do **B** and **C** below.

Yes / No Questions with *be*			Short Answers	
be	Subject pronoun		Affirmative	Negative
Am	I	in this class?	Yes, you **are**.	No, you**'re not**. / No, you **aren't**.
Are	you	a student?	Yes, I **am**.	No, I**'m not**.
Is	he / she		Yes, he **is**.	No, he**'s not**. / No, he **isn't**.
Is	it	her real name?	Yes, it **is**.	No, it**'s not**. / No, it **isn't**.

B  Complete the dialogs. Then practice them with a partner.

1. A: _____*Are you*_____ a student?

   B: Yes, _____.

2. A: _____ English your native language?

   B: No, _____.

3. A: _____ from this city?

   R: No, _____. I'm from Shanghai.

4. A: _____ Chris Hemsworth your favorite actor?

   B: No, _____.

5. A: _____ Taylor Swift your favorite pop singer?

   B: Yes, _____. Her music is great!

6. A: _____ friends with anyone from the US?

   B: Yes, _____. I have a friend who is from New York.

C Ask a partner the six questions in **B**. This time, talk about yourselves.

> Are you a student?

> Yes, I am.

> Is Taylor Swift your favorite pop singer?

> No, she isn't. My favorite is....

5 WRITING

A Write six sentences. Write about your favorite...

actor / actress	sports player	movie
singer	TV show	website

B Write one of your sentences from above on a piece of paper. Give it to your instructor.

My favorite soccer player is Cristiano Ronaldo.

My favorite singer is Rihanna.

6 COMMUNICATION

A Your instructor will give you a classmate's sentence. Ask your classmates *Yes / No* questions. Find the writer of the sentence.

> Is Cristiano Ronaldo your favorite soccer player?

> No, he's not.

> Yes, he is! It's my sentence.

B Repeat **A** with a different sentence.

2COUNTRIES

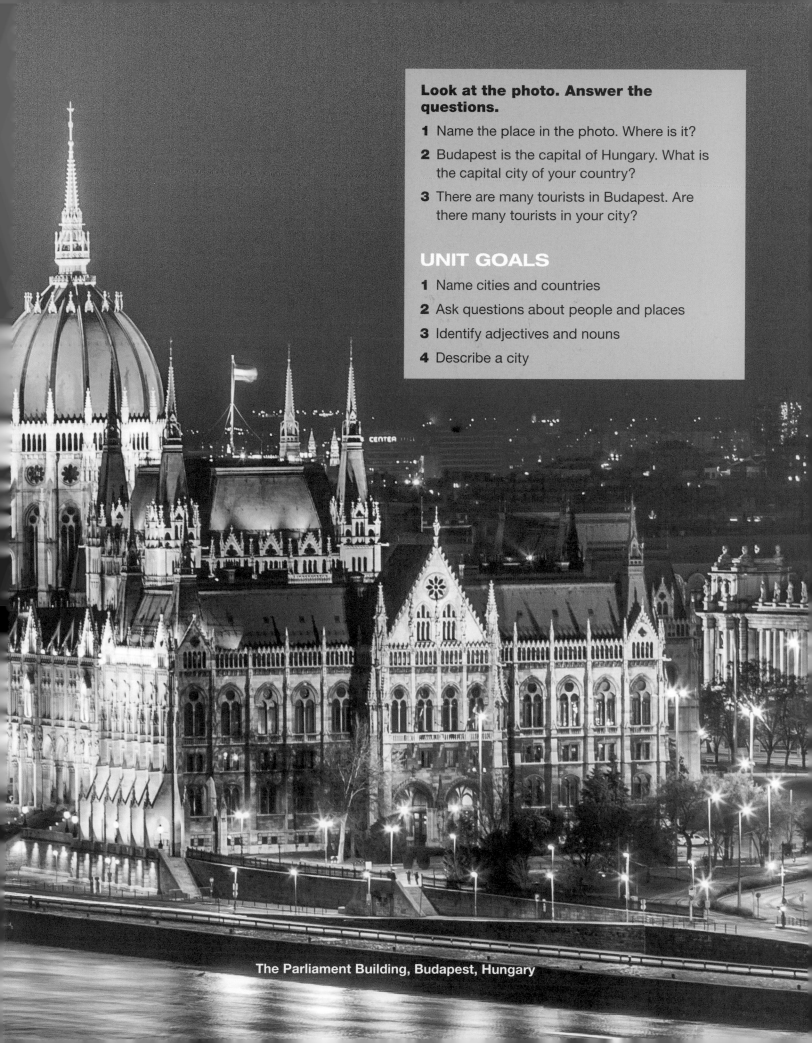

Look at the photo. Answer the questions.

1 Name the place in the photo. Where is it?

2 Budapest is the capital of Hungary. What is the capital city of your country?

3 There are many tourists in Budapest. Are there many tourists in your city?

UNIT GOALS

1 Name cities and countries

2 Ask questions about people and places

3 Identify adjectives and nouns

4 Describe a city

The Parliament Building, Budapest, Hungary

A beach in Southern Thailand

1 **VIDEO** Speeding Around the World in Under Five Minutes

A 🔊 Listen. Say each country after the speaker. **Track 9**

☐ Egypt   ☐ Mexico   ☐ Portugal   ☐ Spain   ☐ the United Kingdom
☐ Japan   ☐ Peru   ☐ South Korea   ☐ Turkey   ☐ the United States

B ▶ Watch the video. Check (✓) the countries in **A** that you see in the video. Two are extra.

C ▶ 🔄 Watch again. Say two other countries in the video. Do you remember any cities? Tell a partner.

D 🔄 Which place in the video is your favorite? Tell a partner.

2 VOCABULARY

Yusef

Mei Li

Ji Ming

Sofia

Diego

Ryan

A 🔊 **Pronunciation: Stressed syllables.** Listen and repeat. Say the countries and nationalities in the chart. **Track 10**

B 🔊 **Pronunciation: Stressed syllables.** Listen and repeat again. Which nationalities have a different syllable stressed than the countries? Circle them in the chart. **Track 10**

The same syllable is stressed	A different syllable is stressed
Bra ZIL Bra ZIL ian	CHI na Chi NESE

C 🔄 Where is each World Cup fan from? What languages do they speak? Tell a partner. Use the words in the chart.

> Yusef is from Turkey.

> Yusef is Turkish. He speaks Turkish.

Country	Nationality
China	(Chinese)
Japan	Japanese
Portugal	Portuguese
Australia	Australian
Brazil	Brazilian
Peru	Peruvian
Korea	Korean
Mexico	Mexican
the United States	American
Spain	Spanish
the United Kingdom	British
Turkey	Turkish

D 🔄 Where are you from? What language(s) do you speak? Tell a partner.

3 LISTENING

Machu Picchu

A 🔊 **Make predictions.** *Where in the World?* is a TV game show. Listen to each clue. Then circle the correct answer. **Track 11**

1. a. the United States b. Canada c. Mexico
2. a. Canada b. Brazil c. the United Kingdom
3. a. Australia b. Argentina c. New Zealand
4. a. France b. the United States c. China
5. a. Brazil b. Chile c. Peru
6. a. Thailand b. Vietnam c. Malaysia

B 🔊 **Check predictions; Listen for details.** Listen. Check your answers in **A**. **Track 12**

✓	That's right. / That's correct.
✗	That's wrong. / That's incorrect.

C 🔄 People from New Zealand are New Zealanders. They are also called "Kiwis." Look at your answers in **A**. Name each nationality.

4 SPEAKING

A 🔊 Listen to the conversation. Where is Ana from? Where is Haru from? **Track 13**

Tokyo, Japan

HARU: Excuse me? Are you in this class?

ANA: Yes, I am. Are you?

HARU: Yeah. Hi, my name's <u>Haru</u>.

ANA: Hi, I'm <u>Ana</u>.

HARU: Great to meet you.

ANA: You, too. So, where are you from, <u>Haru</u>?

HARU: <u>Japan</u>.

ANA: Cool. Which city?

HARU: <u>Tokyo</u>. How about you? Where are you from?

ANA: <u>Bogotá, Colombia</u>.

B 🔁 Now practice the conversation in **A** with a partner. Replace the underlined words with your own information.

SPEAKING STRATEGY

C Think of a famous person. Write his or her information below.

Name: _____

City and country: _____

D 👥 Imagine you are a famous person at a party. Meet three people using the Useful Expressions.

> Hi, I'm Rafael Nadal.

> Hi, Rafa. Where are you from?

> I'm from Spain.

> Really? Which city?

Useful Expressions
Asking where someone is from
Where are you from?
(I'm from) Japan.
Really? Where exactly? Which city?
(I'm from) Tokyo / a small town near Tokyo.
Are you from Colombia?
Yes, I am.
No, I'm from Peru.
Speaking Tip
Where in Japan?
Osaka.

A teahouse in Shanghai, China

5 GRAMMAR

A Turn to page 71. Complete the exercises. Then do **B–E** below.

Questions with *who*			Answers
Who	is / 's	with you?	Tomas (is).

Questions with *where*			Answers
Where	are	you / they?	(I'm / We're / They're) **at** the beach / a museum.
Where	is / 's	Nor?	(She's) **in** London. / **at** her hotel.
		Machu Picchu?	(It's) **in** Peru.

B 🔄 Nor is talking to Sara on the phone. Complete the dialog with *who, where, at,* or *in.* Then practice with a partner.

SARA: Hello?

NOR: <u>Sara</u>? Hi, it's <u>Nor</u>.

SARA: Hi, <u>Nor</u>! _____ are you?

NOR: I'm _____ the UK. Right now, I'm _____ London.

SARA: _____ exactly?

NOR: I'm _____ <u>Buckingham Palace</u>. Oh, and I'm here with a friend.

SARA: Really? _____'s with you?

NOR: <u>Irina</u>, from our English class. She lives _____ <u>London</u> now.

SARA: That's great! Say "Hi" for me.

C 🔄 Make two new conversations with a partner. Replace the underlined parts in **B** with the ideas below.

1. Use your names at the start and one of these two places.
   • Shanghai, China / a teahouse   • Punta Cana, the Dominican Republic / a beach

2. At the end, use a classmate's name.

D 🔄 Repeat Exercise **C**. Use a new city and place. Sit back-to-back with your partner and have the conversation. Try not to read the dialog.

E 🔄 Work with a new partner. Talk about your "phone call" in Exercise **D**. Where is your partner? Who is your partner with?

> Marta is in New York City with Diego. They're at the Statue of Liberty.

6 COMMUNICATION

A 🔄 **Directions:** Play in pairs.

1. Put a marker (a coin, an eraser) on *Start Here*.

2. Take turns. Flip a coin.

    Heads: Move one square.
    Tails: Move two squares.

3. Answer the question. For *Free Question!,* your partner asks you about a city or country.

    Each correct answer = 1 point

4. Finish at square 24. The winner is the person with the most points.

Heads

Tails

Answers are on page 80.

Carnival

FUN FACTS ABOUT RIO DE JANEIRO, BRAZIL

Rio is a **large**, **old** city of 6.5 million people.

Its nickname is "the Marvelous City" because its beaches are **beautiful**, its nightlife is **exciting**, and its people are **friendly**.

Rio is **famous** for…

- Carnival: Every year the streets are **crowded** and **busy** with people from all over Brazil and the world.
- Copacabana: This is a **relaxing** beach. It's also a **popular** place to play soccer.
- Pão de Açúcar: This is a **big** mountain. It is 396 meters (1,300 feet) **tall**. From here, there's a **wonderful** view of the city.

Rio is an **interesting** city and a **fun** place to visit!

Copacabana and Pão de Açúcar

1 VOCABULARY

A   Look at the pictures and read about the city of Rio. Is your city the same or different? Tell a partner. Use the vocabulary words.

> My city isn't large, but it is old.

B   Answer the questions with a partner.

1. Is your city big or small?
2. Is it interesting?
3. Are the people friendly?
4. Are the streets crowded? If yes, where and when?
5. What is your city famous for?
6. What is your favorite place in your city? Why?

Word Bank
Opposites
big, large ↔ **small**
old ↔ **new**
interesting ↔ **boring**

2 LISTENING

Khaju Bridge, Isfahan

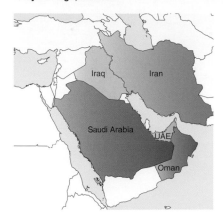

The Grand Bazaar, Isfahan

A 🔁 **Make predictions.** Answer the questions with a partner.

1. Look at the map. Say the countries together. What part of the world is this?

2. Look at the photos. What words describe these places? Use the words from page 24.

B 🔊 Listen to John talk about the city of Isfahan. Where is it? Write your answer: _____.
Track 14

C 🔊 **Listen for details.** Listen. Match the places (1–5) to the words that describe them (a–h). Some will have more than one answer. **Track 15**

1. Iran _____
2. Iranians _____
3. Khaju Bridge _____
4. the main square _____
5. Isfahan _____

a. beautiful   e. wonderful
b. big   f. old
c. famous   g. relaxing
d. friendly   h. interesting

D 🔁 Do you want to visit Isfahan? Why or why not? Tell a partner.

3 READING 🔊 Track 16

A 🔄 In one minute, write down any famous cities and places in your country on a piece of paper. Compare your lists with a partner's. Why are the places famous?

B **Scan for information.** Read the email. Where is Melissa? In which city and country? Follow the steps below to guess.

1. Circle key words.
2. Write your guess:

_____

3. 🔄 Compare your answer with a partner's.
4. Check your answer at the bottom of the next page.

C **Read for details.** Read Melissa's note. Circle T for *True* or F for *False*. Correct the false sentences to make them true.

1. Melissa is in Sydney.   T   F

_____

2. She's on vacation.   T   F

_____

3. She's in a big city.   T   F

_____

4. Long Street is not busy. T   F

_____

5. Penguins are on Table Mountain.   T   F

_____

6. Melissa loves soccer.   T   F

_____

7. Her vacation is fun.   T   F

_____

A GREAT PLACE TO VISIT

Penguins at Boulders Beach

Hi Cary,

Greetings! It's day six of my vacation. I'm in a big city of 3.75 million people. It's very exciting.

Right now I'm in a busy cafe on Long Street. There are a lot of restaurants and shops on Long Street. The streets are very crowded!

There are a lot of interesting things to see and do here. Boulders Beach is beautiful. It's famous for penguins!

There's also Table Mountain. It's a popular place. The view from there is really wonderful.

There are a lot of World Cup soccer stadiums here. Do you like soccer? I don't!

I'm having a great time! Please say "Hi" to everyone in Sydney for me!

Melissa

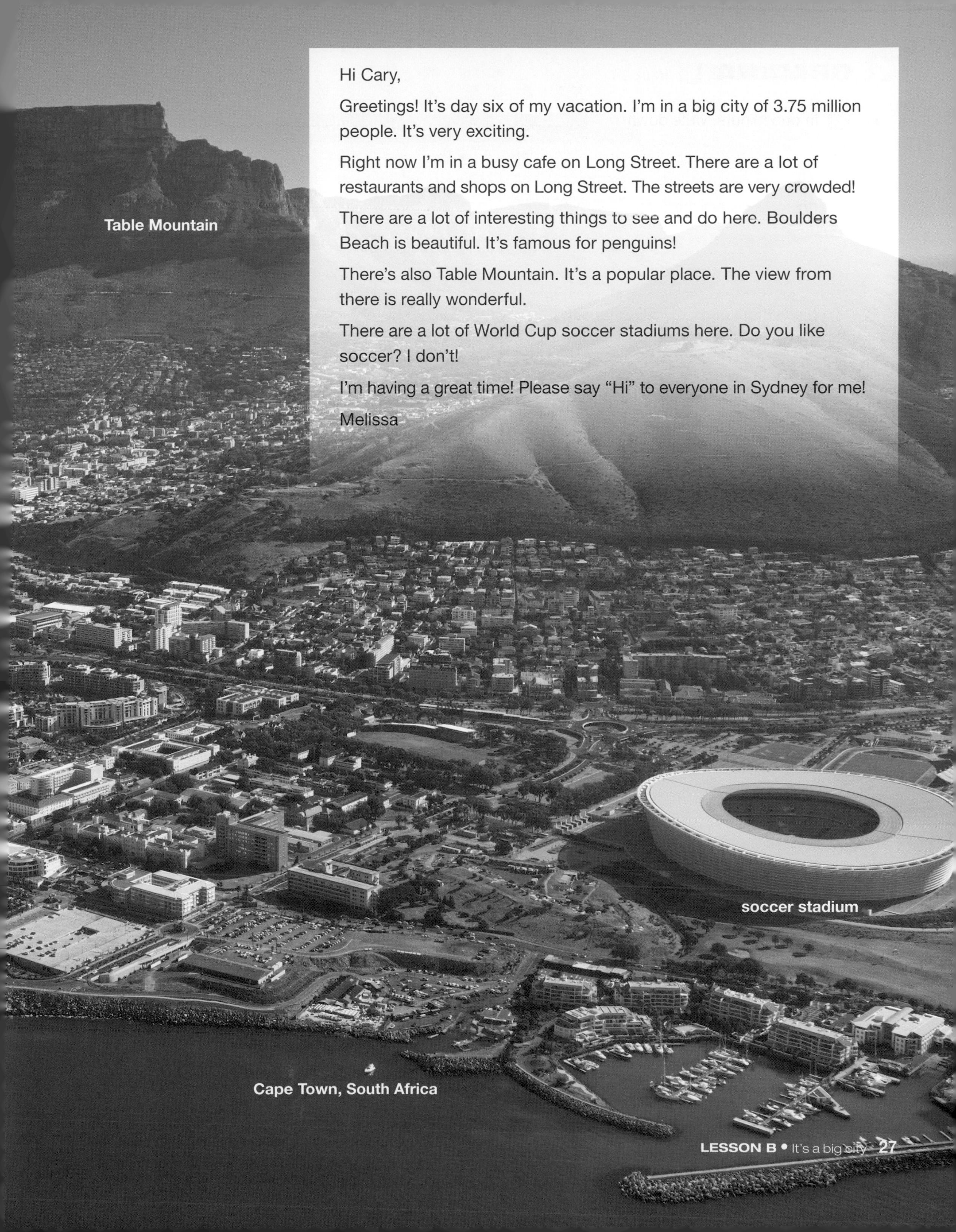

Table Mountain

soccer stadium

Cape Town, South Africa

4 GRAMMAR

Adjectives with *be*							
	be	Adjective			*be*	Adjective	Noun
Your city	**is**	beautiful.	It		**is**	an exciting	city.
The buildings	**are**	old.	There		**are**	many tall	buildings.

A hiker in Arrochar, Scotland

A Turn to page 72. Complete the exercises. Then do **B–E** below.

B 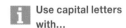 Take turns describing your city with a partner. Use adjectives with *be*.

C 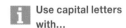 Look at the sentences in the grammar chart above. Work with a partner. Rewrite each one as a question.

Your city is beautiful. → *Is your city beautiful?*

D Read the sentences. On a piece of paper, rewrite each one as a question.

1. The food is good.
2. It's an interesting city.
3. The streets are crowded.
4. It's busy and exciting.
5. The people are friendly.
6. It's famous for music.

E 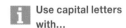 Think of a place. Take turns guessing your partner's place. Ask questions like the ones in **D**.

> Are the streets crowded there?

> No, they aren't.

> Is it a relaxing place?

> Yes, it is.

5 WRITING

A You are going to write about your favorite place. First, answer these questions on a piece of paper.

1. What is the name of your favorite place?
2. Where is it?
3. What are two adjectives that describe it?
4. What is it famous for?

> **i** Use capital letters with...
> • people and place names
> • countries and languages

Bedugul, Bali

B Write about your favorite place. Use your notes in **A**.

My favorite place is Montreal. It's in Canada. People speak English and French there. It's famous for churches and ice hockey. Montreal is busy with people from around the world. The French food is good, too!

C Exchange papers with a partner. Check for capital letters. Do you want to visit your partner's place?

6 COMMUNICATION

A Look at the map and photo. Where is Bali—in which country? Is it a good place for a vacation?

B Where is a good place for a vacation? Write your ideas in the chart under *My idea*.

	My idea	My classmate's idea	My classmate's idea	My classmate's idea
Place				
Where is it?				
How is it there?				

C Interview three classmates. Complete the rest of the chart.

D Choose one place for a vacation. Explain your choice to a partner.

> It's a good place for a vacation. The beaches are beautiful, the people are friendly, and the nightlife is fun.

3 POSSESSIONS

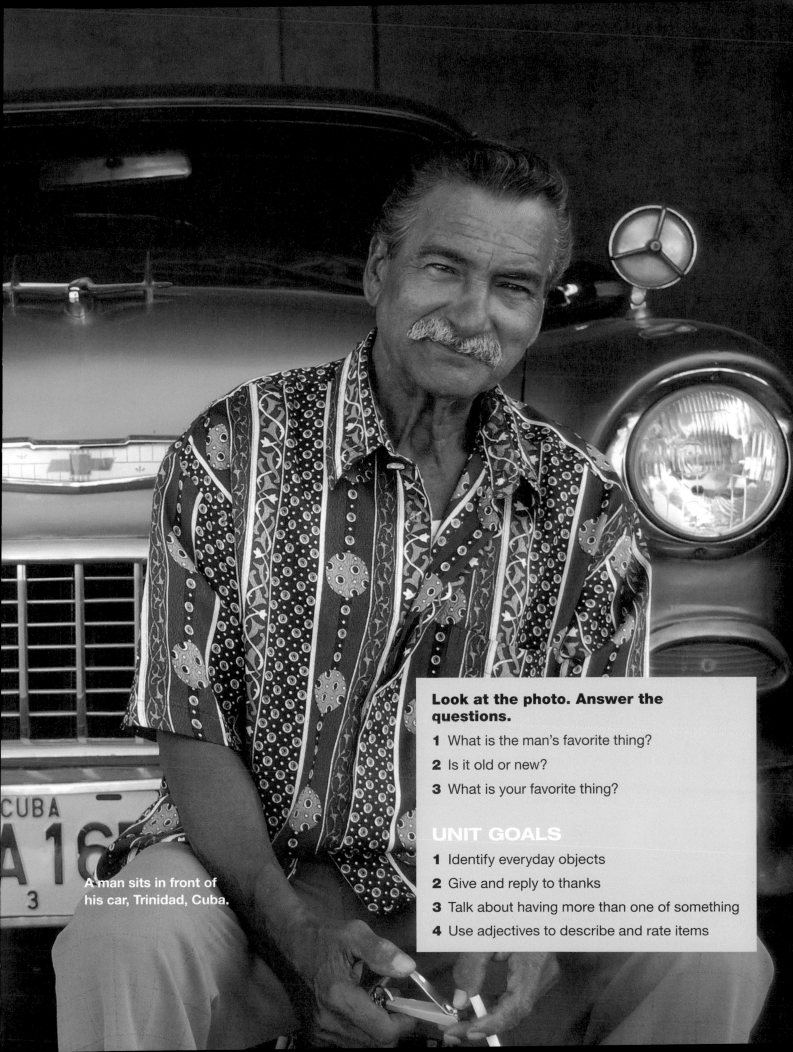

A man sits in front of his car, Trinidad, Cuba.

Look at the photo. Answer the questions.

1 What is the man's favorite thing?

2 Is it old or new?

3 What is your favorite thing?

UNIT GOALS

1 Identify everyday objects

2 Give and reply to thanks

3 Talk about having more than one of something

4 Use adjectives to describe and rate items

1 VIDEO What Do You Carry With You?

A Look at the photo and the title of the video. Guess: What is the video about? Circle your answer. Tell a partner.

a. gifts   b. important items   c. friends

B ▶ Watch the video. Check your answer in **A**.

C ▶ What items are in the video? Check (✓) the ones you see.

☐ a photo   ☐ keys   ☐ a cell phone   ☐ a map
☐ candy   ☐ a computer   ☐ a ring   ☐ a wallet
☐ a book   ☐ a soccer ball   ☐ an apple   ☐ a camera

D What do you carry with you? Tell a partner.

> I always carry a book.

2 VOCABULARY

A Match each item in the list with an item on the website. Write the numbers on the website.

1. a **backpack**
2. a **camera**
3. a **gift card**

4. **headphones**
5. a **wallet**
6. an **expensive watch**

gift link.com   🔍 Search for gifts   HOME | SALE | CUSTOMER SERVICE | 🛒 CART

Gift ideas >> Graduation gifts for students >> Most popular

B 🔄 Look at the gifts. With a partner, ask and answer a question about each one.

What's this?

A watch.

C 🔄 Answer these questions with a partner.

1. What items in **A** do you have?

2. What is the best gift for a student?

3. Which of these gifts is your favorite?

3 LISTENING

A 🔊 **Listen for details.** Listen and circle the correct answers. **Track 17**

1. Sue is Tak's classmate / friend.

2. Tak is buying her a graduation / birthday gift.

3. Sue likes baseball / tennis / soccer.

4. She likes hip-hop / pop music.

Word Bank
birthday = day someone was born
brand = category of products made by a company

B 🔊 **Listen for sequence.** Listen. Number the items as you hear them. (You will not number all of the items.) **Track 18**

a backpack _____   a camera _____

headphones _____   a watch _____

a wallet _____   a gift card _____

C 🔊 Listen. Does Tak buy each item? Why or why not? Check and circle your answers. **Track 19**

1. ☐ buys ☐ doesn't buy   It's a boring / fun gift.

2. ☐ buys ☐ doesn't buy   It's a nice / an expensive gift.

3. ☐ buys ☐ doesn't buy   They're popular / her favorite brand.

4 SPEAKING

A 🔊 👥 Listen to the conversation. Then practice it with two partners. **Track 20**

SUN: Oh, no...

PAULA: What's wrong, Sun?

SUN: My wallet. Where's my <u>wallet</u>?

PAULA: Is it in your pocket?

SUN: Um... no.

PAULA: What about your backpack?

SUN: No, it's not. I can't find it anywhere!

MAN: Hmm... what's this? Excuse me, miss?

SUN: Yes?

MAN: Is this your <u>wallet</u>?

SUN: Yes, it is! Thank you very much!

MAN: You're welcome.

B 👥 Practice the conversation again. Take a different role. Replace the underlined word in **A** to ask about the items below.

key   student ID   bus pass

SPEAKING STRATEGY

C Imagine you lost one of the important items below. Create a short dialog. Thank and reply to each other formally.

D Repeat the dialog in **C**. This time, thank and reply to each other informally.

Useful Expressions		
Giving and replying to thanks		
Saying *Thank you*		**Replies**
Thank you very much.	**formal**	You're welcome.
Thank you.	↕	My pleasure.
Thanks a lot.		Sure, no problem.
Thanks.	**informal**	You bet.

a credit card   a cell phone   a notebook   a laptop

5 GRAMMAR

A Turn to page 73. Complete the exercises. Then do **B** and **C** below.

Spelling Rules for Forming Plural Nouns		
Most plural nouns are formed by adding *s*:	camera → camera**s**	pen → pen**s**
For nouns ending in a <u>vowel</u> + *y* add *s*:	boy → boy**s**	
but For nouns ending in a <u>consonant</u> + *y*, drop the *y* and add *ies*:	dictiona**ry** → dictiona**ries**	
For nouns ending in a <u>vowel</u> + *o* add *s*:	rad**io** → rad**ios**	
but For nouns ending in a <u>consonant</u> + *o*, add *s* with some nouns and *es* with others:	pho**to** → pho**tos**	pota**to** → pota**toes**
For nouns ending in *ch, sh, ss,* or *x*, add *es:*	cla**ss** → cla**sses**	
For nouns ending in *f / fe*, change it to *ve* + *s*:	kni**fe** → kni**ves**	lea**f** → lea**ves**

B 🔊 **Pronunciation: Plural endings.** Listen and repeat. Then practice saying the singular and plural forms of the nouns. **Track 21**

> **Group 1**
> class → classes   wish → wishes
> watch → watches   language → languages
>
> **Group 2**
> backpack → backpacks   laptop → laptops
> notebook → notebooks   wallet → wallets
>
> **Group 3**
> camera → cameras   gift card → gift cards
> key → keys   pen → pens

C 🔄 Read the rules of the guessing game. Then play the game with a partner.

1. Write the number *1* on five pieces of paper.
2. Write the number *2* on five pieces of paper.
3. Mix up the pieces of paper and place them face down.
4. Choose a word from the list in Exercise **B** and pick up a piece of paper.
5. Draw one or two pictures of your word (for example *one pen* or *two backpacks*).
6. Your partner guesses the answer and then spells out the word.

> The answer is backpacks.
> B-A-C-K-P-A-C-K-S.

6 COMMUNICATION

A 🔄 Practice the conversation with a partner.

LUCAS: Oh, let's see.... What's this? Wow, it's a cool watch. Thanks, Jane. I really like it.

JANE: No problem, Lucas. I'm glad you like it.

B 🔄 Practice the conversation again with a different gift idea and way of saying *Thank you*.

When people say *Thank you* for a gift, they also say...		
Thanks.	I really like it / them.	
	I like it / them a lot.	
	It's They're	cool / beautiful / great / nice / perfect.

C Think of a gift. Write the name of the gift on a small piece of paper. Fold the paper.

a watch

sunglasses

D 🔄 Follow these gift-giving steps.

1. Exchange the gifts you wrote in **C** with a partner. Thank your partner. Write the name of the gift in the box below.

2. Exchange the gift you got with a new partner. Then do this three more times. Write each new gift in the box.

Gifts
1. _____
2. _____
3. _____
4. _____
5. _____

E 🔄 Tell a new partner about your gifts. Which is your favorite?

I got sunglasses, a watch, a laptop....

What's your favorite?

The laptop!

1 VOCABULARY

A 🔄 Look at the photo. Read the information. Then circle the correct word with a partner.

1. A pack rat's room is / isn't clean.

2. A pack rat keeps / throws out old things.

3. For a pack rat, only the expensive / cheap and expensive things are important.

B Complete the sentences. Make them true for you.

1. My room is / isn't messy.

2. It's hard / easy to find things in my room.

3. Usually, I keep / throw out old things.

4. True or False for you: Sometimes, I buy something because it's cheap, but I don't use it.

C 🔄 Tell a partner your answers in **B**. Are you similar to Laura?

> My room isn't messy. It's clean and comfortable.

Laura is a "pack rat." There are many old things in her room: clothes, bags, photos. She doesn't use these things anymore. Some of the things are expensive. But some things, like the clothes, are **cheap**. For Laura, they are all **important**. She **keeps** everything!

Laura's room is **messy**, and it's **hard** to find things. For you and me, her room is **uncomfortable**, but not for Laura! She likes it.

The prefix **un** = **not**

Word Bank
Opposites
cheap ↔ expensive
comfortable ↔ uncomfortable
hard ↔ **easy**
important ↔ **unimportant**
keep ↔ **throw out**
messy ↔ **clean**

2 LISTENING

A **Make predictions.** Alison is cleaning her room. She is talking to her friend Mia about the things above. Guess: Which country are these things from? _____

B 🔊 **Listen for gist.** Listen. Number the things above (1, 2, 3) as you hear them. **Track 22**

C 🔊 **Listen for details.** Listen again. Does Alison keep or throw out each thing? Why? Mark the correct answers. **Track 22**

	Alison...	**Why?**
1.	☐ keeps it. ☐ throws it out.	It's clean / cool / old.
2.	☐ keeps it. ☐ throws it out.	It's a(n) nice / interesting / bad photo.
3.	☐ keeps it. ☐ throws it out.	It's from an expensive store.
		a good friend.
		a popular museum.

D 💬 Do you keep any old things? Why? Tell a partner. Give an example.

3 ▶ READING 🔊 Track 23

A 🔄 **Infer information.** Read the title, the sentences under it, and the boxed information. Guess: What is a photographer's most important item? What is an archaeologist's most important item?

B **Scan for information.** Read the article. Then follow the steps below.

1. Circle each person's important item(s).

2. Why is the item important to the person? Underline the answer.

C 🔄 With a partner, explain each person's most important item. Use your answers in **B**.

> Person 1 is Cory Richards. His most important item is....

D 🔄 What item is important to you? Why? Tell a partner. Are any answers the same in your class?

> It's my cell phone. There's a lot of important information on my phone.

Word Bank
GPS
hat
sunscreen

THE ONE THING I CAN'T LIVE WITHOUT

What item is very important to you? Five people from National Geographic share their ideas.

The people at *National Geographic*

A *photographer* takes pictures.

An *archaeologist* and a *paleoanthropologist* find and study very old humans and their cultures.

1 **CORY RICHARDS** is a photographer. A camera and a pencil are his most important items. They are common[1] items, but with these, he takes pictures and writes about his experiences.

2 **CARLTON WARD** is also a photographer. His camera is important to him, but his GPS is important, too. Ward works in different places around the world, and it's easy to get lost.[2] He uses the GPS to get directions.

3 Archaeologist **CHRIS THORNTON** works in places like South Africa and Oman. He is outside a lot. For this reason, his most important item is sunscreen. "It protects[3] my skin," he says.

4 **LEE BERGER** is a paleoanthropologist. He is also outside a lot. But his most important item isn't sunscreen; it's a comfortable hat. "It's my lucky hat," he says. When he wears it, he always finds something interesting.

5 Archaeologist **KUENGA WANGMO** also has a lucky item. It's a bracelet from Bhutan, her home country. It protects her, she says.

Carlton Ward

[1]If something is *common*, many people have it.
[2]If you are *lost*, you don't know where you are.
[3]If something *protects* you, it keeps you safe.

4 GRAMMAR

A Turn to page 74. Complete the exercises. Then do **B–D** below.

this / that / these / those	
What's **this** called in English?	It's a "cell phone."
Is **that** a new phone?	Yes, it is.
Are **these** your keys?	No, they're not.
Are **those** headphones comfortable?	Yes, they are.

B 🔄 Look in your backpack or bag. Put three or four things from it on your desk (for example, your keys, wallet, or phone). Then follow the steps below.

1. Pick up an item on your partner's desk. Ask what it's called in English.

2. Ask one follow-up question about the item.

3. Change roles. Repeat steps 1 and 2.

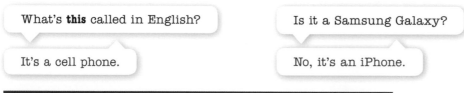

What's **this** called in English?

It's a cell phone.

Is it a Samsung Galaxy?

No, it's an iPhone.

Possible follow-up questions
Is it / Are they (new / comfortable / expensive)?
Is it a(n) (iPhone)?
Where's it from? / Where are they from?
Your idea: _____?

C 🔄 Work with your partner. This time:

1. Point to an item on your partner's desk. Ask what it's called in English.

2. Ask one more question about the item.

3. Change roles. Repeat steps 1 and 2.

What are **those** called in English?

They're cool. Where are they from?

They're sunglasses.

Lotte Department Store.

D 🔄 Repeat **B** and **C** with a new partner. Use items around the classroom.

5 WRITING

A Read a rating of this item. Is it a good phone? Why or why not? Tell a partner.

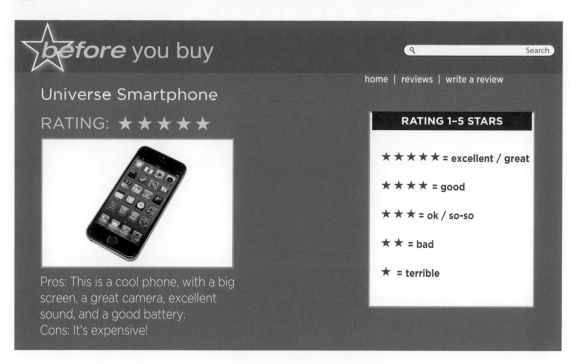

before you buy

home | reviews | write a review

Search

Universe Smartphone

RATING: ★ ★ ★ ★ ★

Pros: This is a cool phone, with a big screen, a great camera, excellent sound, and a good battery.
Cons: It's expensive!

RATING 1–5 STARS

★ ★ ★ ★ ★ = excellent / great

★ ★ ★ ★ = good

★ ★ ★ = ok / so-so

★ ★ = bad

★ = terrible

B Think of a product (a phone, a tablet, a bike, headphones, etc.).

1. What's good about it? Write one or two things. What's bad about it? Write one thing.

2. Find a photo of it online.

6 COMMUNICATION

A Tell four people about your item from above. Show the photo. Then listen and complete the chart below with information about their products.

Product name	Pros	Cons
Example: Universe	The screen is big. The sound is excellent. The battery is good.	It's expensive.
1.		
2.		
3.		
4.		

B Which product from your list in **A** is the best? Why? Tell a new partner.

> The Universe? Oh yeah, that's a good phone.

4 ACTIVITIES

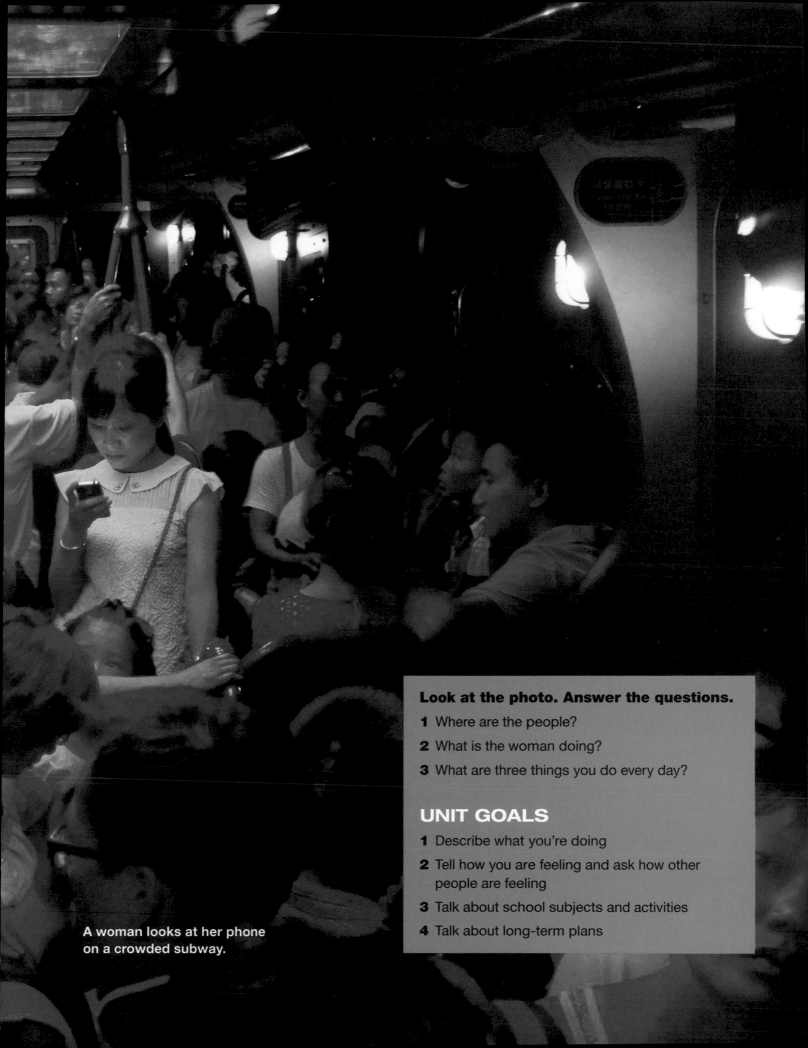

Look at the photo. Answer the questions.

1 Where are the people?

2 What is the woman doing?

3 What are three things you do every day?

UNIT GOALS

1 Describe what you're doing

2 Tell how you are feeling and ask how other people are feeling

3 Talk about school subjects and activities

4 Talk about long-term plans

A woman looks at her phone on a crowded subway.

A group of students sitting outside of a school building

1 VIDEO Day in the Life of a College Student

A ▶ Watch the video with the sound off. Where are these people? What do they do? Write three things.

_____

_____

_____

B ▶ Watch the video again with the sound on. Check your answers.

C What are the people in the video doing? Tell a partner.

2 VOCABULARY

A What are these people doing? Match each sentence with a photo.

1. He's **doing** his homework and **studying** for a test.
2. He's **watching** TV.
3. He's **texting** a friend.
4. She's **exercising** and **listening** to music.
5. He's **talking** on the phone.
6. She's **eating** pizza and **drinking** soda.
7. They're **going** to school.
8. She's **shopping**.

B 🗣 Cover up the sentences. Point to a person and ask your partner a question.

What's he doing?

He's doing his homework.

3 LISTENING

A 🔁 **Pronunciation: Question intonation.** Read the dialog below. Practice it with a partner.

A: How are you[1] doing today?
B: Fine, thanks. How about you[2]?
A: I'm doing great.

[1] Sounds like *How're you*
[2] Sounds like *How 'bout you*

B 🔊 **Pronunciation: Question intonation.** Listen and repeat. **Track 24**

C 🔁 **Make predictions.** You will hear three conversations in **D**. Read the key words from each conversation. What are the people doing in each situation? Tell a partner what you think.

Conversation 1: *popular, expensive, buy*
Conversation 2: *park, running*
Conversation 3: *notebook, pen*

D 🔊 **Listen for gist and details.** Listen to the conversations. What is each person doing? Circle the correct answer. **Track 25**

1. A   B   C
2. A   B   C
3. A   B   C

E 🔁 Check your answers with a partner.

4 SPEAKING

A 🔊 💬 Listen to the conversation. Then answer the questions with a partner.
Track 26

1. What is Shinja doing? What is Luis doing?
2. How is Shinja? How is Luis?

SHINJA: Hello?

LUIS: Hey, Shinja. It's Luis.

SHINJA: Hi, Luis. How are you doing?

LUIS: Fine. How about you?

SHINJA: So-so.

LUIS: Yeah? What's wrong?

SHINJA: I'm waiting for the bus. It's late!

LUIS: Sorry to hear that.

SHINJA: What are you doing, Luis?

LUIS: Not much. I'm watching TV.

B 💬 Practice the conversation in **A** with a partner.

SPEAKING STRATEGY

C 💬 Complete the dialogs below. Use the Useful Expressions to help you. Then practice the dialogs with a partner.

Useful Expressions	
Greeting people and asking how they are	
Positive ☺	A: Hi, Sara. How are you doing? B: Fine. / OK. / All right. / Not bad. How about you? A: I'm fine, thanks.
Negative ☹	A: Hi, Yuki. How's it going? B: So-so. / Not so good. A: Really? / Yeah? What's wrong? B: I'm waiting for the bus. It's late!

1. A: Hi, _____. How _____?
   B: _____ good.
   A: Really? _____?
   B: I'm studying for a test. It's hard!

2. A: Hi, _____. How _____?
   B: Fine. How _____?
   A: All _____. What _____?
   B: Not much. I'm reading a book.

D 🔾 Ask four people in your class how they are doing today.

5 GRAMMAR

A Turn to page 75. Complete the exercise. Then do **B** and **C** below.

The Present Continuous Tense: Affirmative and Negative Statements				
Subject pronoun	**be**	**(not)**	**verb + -ing**	**Contractions with be**
I	**am**	(not)	**working.**	I am = I'm; I am not = I'm not
You	**are**			you are = you're; you are not = you're not / you aren't
He / She / It	**is**			she is = she's; she is not = she's not / she isn't
We / They	**are**			we are = we're; we are not = we're not / we aren't

B Look at picture A below. What are the people doing? On a piece of paper, write five sentences. Use the present continuous tense.

C ⟳ Work with a partner. Look at pictures A and B. Point to a person and ask a question. Find the differences in the pictures.

> What's he doing?

> In picture A, he's talking on the phone.

> But in picture B, he isn't talking on the phone. He's....

6 COMMUNICATION

A Follow the steps below.

1. Get into groups of four. Read the actions. Look up any words you don't know.

dancing to rap music	studying for an exam
exercising at the gym	talking to a boyfriend or girlfriend
playing soccer	texting a friend
playing video games	waiting for the subway
reading a funny book	walking to school
shopping for a graduation gift	watching a sad TV show
sleeping late	working at an office

2. Write each action above on a piece of paper. Mix up the pieces of paper and place them face down.

3. One student takes a piece of paper but doesn't show the others. The student has one minute to act out the action. What is he or she doing? The other three students have one minute to guess by asking *Yes / No* questions. If they guess correctly, the group gets a point.

   > Are you playing soccer?

4. Take turns as the actor and repeat step 3 until you use all the slips of paper. Which group has the most points?

Rules

1. You cannot make any sounds when you are acting out the action.

2. You cannot point to other objects as clues. You *can* point to people if they get part of the answer.

B Play the game again. Make slips of paper and use your own ideas.

LESSON B AT SCHOOL

My name is Luis and **I go to** Simon Bolivar University in Caracas, Venezuela. **I'm studying** music with *El Sistema*, a national music program. **I'm taking classes** like math, science, and history, too. Also, this term, **I'm preparing for** the college entrance exam.

1 VOCABULARY

A 🔄 Which subjects and majors from the chart do you know? Tell a partner. Add one more idea. Then tell the class.

B 🔄 Read about the student above. Answer the questions with a partner.

1. Where is Luis a student?
2. What is he studying?
3. What classes is he taking?
4. What is he preparing for?

C 🔄 Tell a partner about yourself. Use some or all of the sentences below.

I'm a student at…. / I go to….   My favorite subjects are….

I'm majoring in….   I'm preparing for the… exam.

I'm taking a… class.   I work in….

> I'm taking an art class this term.

> ℹ️ You can also say:
> *I go to / I'm a student at….*
> *I'm studying / I'm majoring in* IT at the University of Lima.

School subjects and college majors
art
business
engineering
graphic design
history
information technology (IT)
law
math
nursing
science
🧳 tourism / hospitality

52 UNIT 4 ● Activities

2 LISTENING

A 🔄 **Make predictions.** What classes are shown by the photos? Tell a partner.

B 🔊 **Distinguish speakers.** What class is each man taking? Match each speaker (1, 2, or 3) with a photo. **Track 27**

C 🔊 **Listen for details.** Read the choices below. Then listen again. Circle the <u>two</u> true answers in each sentence. **Track 27**

1. He's _____.   a. a good artist   b. majoring in art   c. taking the class for fun
2. He's _____.   a. working in a   b. trying to get a   c. taking three classes
                        hotel   better job
3. He's _____.   a. not having fun   b. preparing for a   c. trying to lose weight
                        in class   class

D 🔄 Answer the questions with a partner.

1. Point to a picture above. What class is each man taking?
   Why is he taking the class? Use your answers in **B** and **C** to explain.

2. Are you (or someone you know) taking any of these classes? Why?

> He's taking....

> He's trying to....

3 READING 🔊 Track 28

A Look at the photos and captions. Where is Nicolas Ruiz studying this term?

B **Identify main ideas.** Read the interview. Write each question in the correct place to complete it.
Where are you living?
So, are you enjoying Hong Kong?
How's your Chinese?
Which classes are you taking?
So, how's it going?

C **Infer meaning.** Find the words in *italics* below in the reading. Then circle the correct words.
1. A *roommate* is a person you study / live with.
2. If something is *improving*, it is / isn't getting better.
3. *I'm having a great time* means someone is / isn't having fun.

D 🔁 **Find key details.** Read the interview aloud with a partner. Then answer the questions on a piece of paper.
1. What school is Nicolas studying at this term? Why is he going to this school?
2. Where is he living?
3. What classes is he taking?
4. How is he doing in his language class?
5. Is he enjoying Hong Kong? Why or why not?

E 🔁 Imagine you can study in another country. What do you want to learn? Make a new interview with a partner.

> So, Kenji, tell our readers about yourself.

> I'm from Tokyo. This term, I'm studying at the Fashion Institute of Technology in New York.

STUDY ABROAD

People gather in downtown Hong Kong at night.

In this issue of *Study Abroad* magazine, Emma Moore is talking to Nicolas Ruiz, a student from Argentina. He's studying in Hong Kong this term.

Emma: So, Nicolas, tell our readers a little about yourself.

Nicolas: Well, I'm from Argentina. At home, I'm a student at the University of Buenos Aires. This term, I'm studying at the University of Science and Technology, here in Hong Kong.

Emma: Why this school?

Nicolas: Well, I'm majoring in business, and the University of Science and Technology has a great business school.[1]

Emma: 1. _____

Nicolas: Great! The classes are really interesting, and I'm learning a lot. There are also students from all over the world here.

Emma: 2. _____

Nicolas: I'm in a dorm[2] with a roommate. He's from Malaysia and he's really nice.

Emma: Glad to hear it. So, tell us about school. 3. _____

Nicolas: I'm taking three business classes and one Chinese class.

Emma: 4. _____

Nicolas: It's OK. My speaking is improving. Now I can talk to people outside of school.

Emma: Excellent. 5. _____

Nicolas: Oh, yeah. I'm having a great time. There's a lot to do and see. It's a really exciting and beautiful city.

Emma: That's wonderful. Thanks a lot for your time, Nicolas, and good luck with your studies!

[1]At a university, there are many *schools* (the school of business, education, law, etc.). Each school focuses on one area of study.

[2]A *dormitory (dorm)* is a school building where students live.

Hong Kong University of Science and Technology

A Turn to pages 76–77. Complete the exercises. Then do **B** and **C** below.

The Present Continuous Tense: Extended Time	
Question	**Response**
What **are** you **doing** these days / nowadays?	I'**m studying** in Hong Kong this term.
Are you **enjoying** Hong Kong?	Yes, I'**m having** a great time!

B 🔁 Two old friends meet on the street. Complete the conversation with the present continuous tense. Use the words given. Then practice with a partner.

ZACK: Hey, Leo!

LEO: Hi, Zack!

ZACK: How are you doing?

LEO: I'm all right. How about you?

ZACK: Not bad. So, (1. what / you / do) _____ these days?

LEO: (2. I / study) _____ at State University.

ZACK: Really? (3. What / you / major) _____ in?

LEO: Graphic design. What about you? (4. you / work) _____ or (5. you / go) _____ to school?

ZACK: Both. (6. I / work) _____ part-time at a cafe. (7. I / take) _____ two classes at City College this term, too.

LEO: (8. What / you / study) _____?

ZACK: Photography and art history.

LEO: (9. you / enjoy) _____ the classes?

ZACK: Yeah. They're fun and (10. I / learn) _____ a lot.

C 🔁 Make a new conversation. Use your own information in **B**.

5 WRITING

A Complete the interview with your answers.

Studying English: Interview Questions

1. Why are you studying English?

    ☐ I'm doing it for fun.   ☐ I'm doing it for my job.

    ☐ I want to travel.   ☐ I'm preparing for an exam.

    ☐ I'm majoring in English.   ☐ Other: _____

2. What are you learning in your English class these days?

    _____

    _____

3. How are you doing in your English class? Is your English improving?

    _____

    _____

4. Outside of class, how are you practicing English?

    _____

    _____

---

6 COMMUNICATION

A Interview three people. Use questions 1–4 in **Writing A**. Write each person's answers on a piece of paper.

> Why are you studying English?

> Is your English improving?

> I'm preparing for the TOEFL.

> My speaking is, but my listening....

B Work with a new partner. Tell your partner about the three people you interviewed. Use (but don't read) your notes. Which answers are the most popular in your class?

> Juan and Jin Soo are preparing for the TOEFL.

EXPANSION ACTIVITIES

1 STORYBOARD

A Adriano and Li Mei are students. It's the first day of class. Complete the conversations.

B 👥 In groups of three, practice the conversations.

C 👥 Switch roles and practice the conversations again.

2 SEE IT AND SAY IT

A   Look at the picture. Find these things.

a cell phone	a watch	a backpack	keys	a camera
sunglasses	a skateboard	a book	a hat	a person's name

B   🗣 Talk about the picture with a partner.

- Where are the people?

- Where are they from? Who is / isn't on vacation?

- Point to three things in the picture. Ask and answer:
  What's this / What are these called in English?

- Ask one more question about the picture.

C   🗣 Choose two people in the picture.
Role-play a short conversation between the people.

> Excuse me? Are these your keys?

> Yes, they are. Thanks!

3 COUNTRIES AND NATIONALITIES

A Read the clues. Complete the crossword puzzle. Check your answers with a partner.

Across

1. The capital of _____ is Berlin.
4. Beijing is the capital of _____.
6. The Queen of England lives in this city. _____
7. A person from Brazil is _____.
9. The capital of Canada is _____.
10. The _____ Opera House is in Australia.

Down

2. In this country, people speak Spanish. _____
3. Tokyo is the capital of _____.
5. _____ is the capital of South Korea.
7. A person from the United Kingdom is _____.
8. This city is the capital of Italy. _____

4 COME IN TODAY!

A Listen to the announcement. Then complete the sentences. **Track 29**

1. Everything at Good Buys is on sale for _____.

   a. one day
   b. two days
   c. three days
   d. one week

2. Good Buys is a(n) _____ store.

   a. book
   b. online
   c. clothing
   d. electronics

3. At the sale, you get _____.

   a. a phone for 25 dollars
   b. free headphones
   c. 25 dollars
   d. a free phone

Word Bank
free = costing no money
sale = when an item costs less money

5 SMALL TOWN, BIG CITY

A Look at the pictures. Use the words in the box and compare the two places. Take turns with a partner.

> The city is big and....
> The town isn't. It's....

beautiful	big	boring	busy	crowded
exciting	fun	interesting	old	relaxing

B Which place do you like—the small town or the big city? Why?

C Tell your partner about a famous town or city. Your partner guesses the city.

> This city is very exciting. It's a big city. It's in Argentina.

> Is it Buenos Aires?

6 STORYBOARD

A Tony and Paloma are in a cafe. Complete the conversation.

B 🔁 Practice the conversation with a partner.

C 🔁 Change roles and practice the conversation again.

7 SEE IT AND SAY IT

A Look at the picture of the food court. Answer the questions.

1. What food and drinks are healthy?
2. What food and drinks are unhealthy?
3. What food and drinks do you like?
4. Look at the people. What are they doing?

B Imagine you are in the food court. Follow the directions.

1. Choose a place and order some food.

    Student A: You are the server. Ask your partner for his or her order.

    Student B: Order something to eat and drink.

2. Change roles and repeat step 1.

C Think of a new restaurant for the food court. Answer the questions.

1. What kind of restaurant is it (Korean, Italian, Mexican, etc.)?
2. What is your new restaurant called? Give it a name.
3. What food and drinks are on the menu? Make a list.

D Share your ideas in **C** with another pair.

8 ODD WORD OUT

A 🔄 Look at the groups of words. Circle the one that's different in each group. Tell your partner.

> In number 1, *teacher* is different.

1. mother   father   (teacher)   daughter
2. study   go to school   do homework   get married
3. math   test   business   nursing
4. sausage   breakfast   lunch   dinner
5. rice   soup   meal   chicken
6. mother   sister   aunt   nephew
7. listening to   studying for   majoring in   preparing for
8. bad for you   high in sugar   unhealthy   tastes good

9 HE SPEAKS SPANISH

A 🔄 Look at the picture. What things does this person have in his backpack? Tell a partner.

> He's got a dictionary in his backpack.

B What do you know about this person from the things in his backpack? Make sentences. Use the verbs in parentheses.

1. (be) _His name is Brian Hughes_ .
2. (speak) _____ .
3. (be) _____ .
4. (go) _____ .
5. (like) _____ .
6. (play) _____ .
7. (have) _____ .
8. (study) _____ .

C 🔄 Take four or five things from your backpack or purse and put them on your desk. Then look at your partner's things. What do you know about your partner from his or her things? Ask your partner questions.

> You have keys. Do you drive?

> No, I don't. These are my house keys.

10 NUMBERS GAME

1. Write numbers between 11 and 100 in your BINGO chart.

2. When you hear a number that's in your chart, write an X over it.

3. When all your numbers have an X, say *Bingo!* Be the first person, and you are the winner!

11 WHAT'S WRONG?

A Are these sentences true or false? Write *T* or *F*. Correct the underlined words and numbers to make the false sentences true.

i	+ plus
	– minus
	= equals

_____ 1. Your father's sister is your <u>cousin</u>.

_____ 2. 37 + 22 = <u>sixty</u>.

_____ 3. Your father's sister is your <u>aunt</u>.

_____ 4. Your uncle's son is your <u>sister</u>.

_____ 5. 100 – 24 = <u>seventy-six</u>.

_____ 6. Your aunt's son is your <u>nephew</u>.

_____ 7. Here is a pattern: three, six, nine, twelve, <u>fourteen</u>, eighteen, twenty-one, twenty-four.

_____ 8. Your parents are divorced. Your father marries again. His new wife is your <u>stepmother</u>.

B Check your answers at the bottom of the page. You get one point for each correct answer. How many points do you have?

1. F; aunt, 2. F; 59, 3. T, 4. F; cousin, 5. T, 6. F; cousin 7. F; fifteen, 8. T

LANGUAGE SUMMARIES

UNIT 1 INTRODUCTIONS

LESSON A

Vocabulary

classmate
email address
female / male
first name / last name
letters of the alphabet: A B C D E
  F G H I J K L M N O P Q R S T U
  V W X Y Z
Mr. / Ms. (Mrs. / Miss)
nickname
numbers 0–10: zero, one, two, three,
  four, five, six, seven, eight, nine, ten
phone number
student ID number
teacher

Speaking Strategy

Introducing yourself
Hi, what's your name?
  Hi, my name is Liling.
  I'm Liling. / It's Liling.
  I'm Alberto, but please call
  me Beto.
(It's) nice to meet you.
  (It's) nice to meet you, too.

How do you spell that /
your (last) name?
  It's (spelled) P-O-R-T-E-R.
What's your name?
  I'm Liling. / It's Liling.

LESSON B

Vocabulary

actor / actress
artist
author / writer
favorite (TV show)
**friend / be friends with
  (someone)**
movie
**music (classical, pop, rap,
  rock)**
(soccer) player
singer
**sport (baseball, basketball,
  soccer, tennis)**
team

UNIT 2 COUNTRIES

LESSON A

Vocabulary

(capital) city
country
nationality
(on) vacation

Argentina → Argentinean
Australia → Australian
Brazil → Brazilian
Canada → Canadian
Colombia → Colombian
Chile → Chilean
China → Chinese
Egypt → Egyptian
France → French
Japan → Japanese
Korea → Korean
Mexico → Mexican
New Zealand → New Zealander,
  Kiwi
Peru → Peruvian

Portugal → Portuguese
Spain → Spanish
Thailand → Thai
Turkey → Turkish
**the United Kingdom (the UK)
  → British**
**the United States (the US) →
  American**
Vietnam → Vietnamese

Speaking Strategy

Asking where someone is from
Where are you from?
  (I'm from) Japan.
Really? Where exactly? Which city? /
  Where in Japan?
    (I'm from) Tokyo / a small town
    near Tokyo.
Are you from Colombia?
  Yes, I am.
  No, I'm from Peru.

LESSON B

Vocabulary

beautiful
big
boring
boring
busy
crowded
exciting
famous
friendly
fun
interesting
large
new
old
popular
relaxing
small
tall
wonderful

UNIT **3** POSSESSIONS

LESSON A

Vocabulary

backpack
bus pass
camera
cell phone
credit card
gift card
headphones
(student) ID
key
laptop
notebook
sunglasses
wallet
(expensive) watch

Speaking Strategy

**Giving and replying
  to thanks**
Thank you very much.
  You're welcome.
Thank you.
  My pleasure.
Thanks a lot.
  Sure, no problem.
Thanks.
  You bet.

LESSON B

Vocabulary

cheap ↔ expensive / valuable
comfortable ↔ uncomfortable
hard ↔ easy
important ↔ unimportant
keep ↔ throw out
messy ↔ clean

excellent / great
good
OK / so-so
bad
terrible

LESSON A

Vocabulary

do (homework)
dorm
drink (soda)
eat (pizza)
exercise
go (to school)
have a great time
improve
listen (to music)
roommate
shop
study (for a test)
talk (on the phone)
term
text (a friend)
watch TV

Speaking Strategy

Greeting people and asking how they are

Positive response
A: Hi, (Sara). How are you doing?
B: Fine. / OK. / All right. / Not bad. How about you?
A: I'm fine, thanks.

Negative response
A: Hi, (Yuki). How's it going?
B: So-so. / Not so good.
A: Really? / Yeah? What's wrong?
B: I'm waiting for the bus. It's late!

LESSON B

Vocabulary

School subjects and college majors*
art
business
engineering
graphic design
history
information technology (IT)
law
math
nursing
science
tourism / hospitality

*A *school subject* is an area of study. Your *major* is your main subject of study in college.

Talking about your studies
Where do you go to school?
I go to / I'm a student at the Fashion Institute of Technology.

What are you studying?
I'm studying music / medicine.
I'm majoring in business.
I'm preparing for the college entrance exam.

What classes are you taking?
I'm taking a test-prep **class**. /
I'm taking two business **classes**.

UNIT **1** INTRODUCTIONS

LESSON A

Subject Pronouns with *be*			
Subject pronoun	***be***		**Subject pronoun contractions with *be***
I	**am**		I am = I'm
You	**are**	a student.	you are = you're
He / She	**is**		he is = he's / she is = she's
We / They	**are**	students.	we are = we're / they are = they're
It	**is**	a book.	it is = it's

Possessive Adjectives with *be*			
Possessive adjective		***be***	
My			
Your	last name	**is**	Smith.
His / Her			
Our / Their			
Its	title	**is**	*World Link.*

A Complete each sentence with the correct form of the verb *be*.

1. She _____ a teacher.
2. It _____ an ID card.
3. You _____ my classmate.
4. I _____ here.

B Look at the underlined words. Then write the correct subject pronoun.

1. <u>Yuki and Beto</u> are here.
   _____ ___ are here.
2. <u>My ID card</u> is at home.
   _____ is at home.
3. <u>Lily</u> is at school.
   _____ is at school.
4. <u>Carlos</u> is at home.
   _____ is at home.

C Complete the sentences with the correct subject pronoun or possessive adjective.

1. _____ is a teacher. _____ name is Mr. Porter.
2. _____ are my cousins. _____ last name is Novak.
3. _____ name is Yukiko. _____ nickname is Yuki.
4. _____ is a teacher. _____ name is Ms. Groves.

D Rewrite each sentence on a separate piece of paper. Use a contraction.

1. I am a student.
2. You are my classmate.
3. She is a teacher.
4. It is an ID card.
5. They are my classmates.
6. He is a student.

LESSON B

Yes / No Questions with *be*			Short Answers	
be	Subject pronoun		Affirmative	Negative
Am	I	in this class?	Yes, you are.	No, you**'re not**.* / No, you **aren't**.
Are	you	a student?	Yes, I am.	No, **I'm not**.
Is	he / she		Yes, he is.	No, he**'s not**.* / No, he **isn't**.
Is	it	her real name?	Yes, it is.	No, it**'s not**.* / No, it **isn't**.
Are	we	in this class?	Yes, we are.	No, we**'re not**.* / No, we **aren't**.
Are	they	students?	Yes, they are.	No, they**'re not**.* / No, they **aren't**.

*In spoken English, this negative form is more common.

A   Read each question. Circle the correct answer.

1. Is your name John?   a. No, it's not.   b. No, I'm not.
2. Are you from Canada?   a. No, you're not.   b. No, I'm not.
3. Is Ms. Kim the teacher?   a. Yes, she is.   b. Yes, it is.
4. Are you friends with Jane? a. Yes, I am.   b. Yes, I'm friends.
5. Am I late for class?   a. No, it's not.   b. No, you aren't.
6. Are Yuki and Carlos your friends?   a. Yes, we are.   b. No, they're not.

Dae Sung ("Danny") Park

His good friends Vanessa and Milo

B   Look at the photos. Complete the questions and answers. Then ask and answer them with a partner.

1. __Is__ his nickname Dae Sung?   ___No___, it's ___Danny___.
2. _____ baseball _____ sport?   No, _____. _____ is his favorite.
3. _____ Vanessa and Milo his friends?   _____.
4. _____ Vanessa his girlfriend?   _____, they're just friends.
5. _____ you friends with Danny?   No, _____.

70 GRAMMAR NOTES

UNIT 2 COUNTRIES

LESSON A

Questions with *who*			Answers	
Who	is 's	he / she ?	He's / She's my classmate.	*Who* asks about people.
		from Mexico? with you?	Tomas (is).	
	are	you? they?	(I'm) Sara. (They're) my friends.	

Questions with *where*			Answers	
Where	are	you / they?	(I'm / We're / They're) **at** school / work / home. **at** the beach / a museum.	*Where* asks about a place. Use *at* + a place. Use *in* / *from* + a city or country.
Where	is 's	Nor?	(She's) **in** London / **at** her hotel.	
		Machu Picchu?	(It's) **in** Peru.	
		Ryan from?	(He's) **from** Australia.	

A Complete the questions and answers with *who, where, in,* or *at* and information from the chart.

Name	Hometown	Where is he or she now?
Emma ♀	Berlin, Germany	on vacation / Mexico
Hisham ♂	Rabat, Morocco	on vacation / Italy
Jun ♂	Beijing, China	Mei's house
Mei ♀	Beijing, China	home
Tim ♂	Toronto, Canada	work / New York City

1. __Who__ is from Rabat?   Hisham is.

2. _____'s Rabat?   It's _____ Morocco.

3. Where is Hisham now?   He's _____.

4. _____ is Emma from?   She's _____.

5. Who's _____ the US now?   _____ _.

6. _____ exactly is Tim?   He's _____ work _____ New York City.

7. Where are Mei and Jun?   They _____.

8. Who's on vacation now?   _____.

B Write three new *who* or *where* questions about the information in the chart. Ask a partner the questions.

LESSON B

Adjectives with *be*			
	be	**Adjective**	
Your city	**is**	beautiful.	Adjectives are words that describe nouns.
The buildings	**are**	old.	Adjectives follow *be*.
Carnival	**is**	fun and loud.	Use *and* to join two adjectives.

	be		**Adjective**	**Noun**	
It	**is**	an	exciting	city.	Adjectives can come before nouns.
There	**are**	many	tall	buildings.	Use *a* or *an* before singular nouns.

A Circle the adjectives and underline the nouns.

  1. It's a crowded place.

  2. Are you a busy person?

  3. They are tall and beautiful.

  4. She's a friendly teacher.

  5. Our street is busy and interesting.

  6. My small town is famous for good food.

B Put the words in parentheses into the sentences. Write the new sentences.

  1. He's English teacher. (an)

  _____.

  2. The restaurant is small friendly. (and)

  _____.

  3. That student is in class. (new)

  _____.

  4. It's a city of five million people. (large)

  _____.

  5. There's a view from the mountain. (wonderful)

  _____.

  6. It's a big city with the feeling of a town. (small)

  _____.

UNIT 3 POSSESSIONS

LESSON A

Singular and Plural Count Nouns				
It's	**an**	ID card.		Count nouns have singular (= one thing) and plural (= two or more things) forms.
I'm	**a**	student.		
There are ten		students	here.	Use *a* or *an* before singular count nouns only.

When the singular noun begins with a consonant sound, use *a*.
When the singular noun begins with a vowel sound, use *an*.

Spelling Rules for Forming Plural Nouns		
Most plural nouns are formed by adding *s*:	camera → camera**s**	pen → pen**s**
For nouns ending in a <u>vowel</u> + *y* add *s*:	b**oy** → boy**s**	
but For nouns ending in a <u>consonant</u> + *y*, drop the *y* and add *ies*:	dictiona**ry** → dictionar**ies**	
For nouns ending in a <u>vowel</u> + *o* add *s*:	ra**dio** → radio**s**	
but For nouns ending in a <u>consonant</u> + *o*, add *s* with some nouns and *es* with others:	pho**to** → photo**s**	pota**to** → potato**es**
For nouns ending in the *ch, sh, ss,* or *x* sounds, add *es*:	cla**ss** → class**es**	
For nouns ending in *f* or *fe*, change it to *ve* + *s*:	kni**fe** → kni**ves**	leaf → lea**ves**

A 🔁 In your notebook, complete the sentences with the words below. With a partner, practice saying them aloud without looking at your book. Remember to use *a* or *an* for singular words.

1. It's _____.   2. They're _____.

backpack	city	gift card	notebook	teacher
knife	credit card	student ID	pen	umbrella
potato	dictionary	key	photo	wallet
cell phone	email address	laptop	student	watch

B 🔁 Complete the sentences with the singular or plural form of the noun in parentheses. Then ask and answer the questions with a partner.

1. What's in your backpack?

   There's (cell phone) _____, (laptop) _____, and (bus pass) _____.

2. What's in your wallet?

   There's (student ID) _____, two (photo) _____, and two (credit card) _____.

3. What's on your desk?

   There are three (pen) _____, (notebook) _____, and two (dictionary) _____.

LESSON B

this / that / these / those		
A: What's **this** called in English? B: It's (called) a "cell phone."	A: Bill, **this** is my friend Nadia. B: Hi, Nadia. Nice to meet you.	Use **this** to talk about a thing or person near you.
A: Is **that** a new phone? B: Yes, it is.	A: Who's **that** (over there)? B: That's my friend Leo.	Use **that** to talk about a thing or person away from you.
A: Are **these** your keys? B: No, they're not.	A: Yuki, **these** are my parents. B: Nice to meet you.	Use **these** to talk about two or more things or people near you.
A: **Those** headphones are cool. B: Yeah, they are.	A: What are **those**? B: They're my new earrings.	Use **those** to talk about two or more things or people away from you.

A Look at the photos. Complete the questions and answers.

1. A: Is _____ your new tablet?
   B: Yes, _it is_.
   A: It's nice.

2. A: Excuse me! Are _____ your keys?
   B: Yes, _____.
      Thanks.

3. A: Who's _____?
   B: My teacher. Let's go and say hello.

4. A: Are _____ your sunglasses over there?
   B: No, _____. My sunglasses are in my backpack.

5. A: Eva, _____ is Bill.
   B: Hi, Bill. Nice to meet you.

B 🔁 Practice the dialogs in **A** with a partner.

LESSON A

The Present Continuous Tense: Affirmative and Negative Statements				
Subject pronoun	***be***	***(not)***	**verb + *-ing***	**Contractions with *be***
I	**am**	(not)	**working.**	I am = I'm; I am not = I'm not
You	**are**			you are = you're; you are not = you're not / you aren't
He / She / It	**is**			she is = she's; she is not – she's not / she isn't
We / They	**are**			we are = we're; we are not = we're not / we aren't

The Present Continuous Tense: *Wh-* Questions and Answers and *Yes / No* Questions and Answers				
Question word	***be***	**subject**	**verb + *-ing***	**Answers**
What	**are**	you	**doing?**	(I'm) **exercising.**
	is	he		(He's) **exercising.**
	are	they		(They're) **exercising.**
Where	**are**	you	**sitting?**	(We're) **sitting** in the front.
	be	**subject**	**verb + *-ing***	**Short answers**
	Are	you	**studying?**	Yes, I am.
				No, I'm not. I'm **texting.**
	Is	she		Yes, she is.
				No, she's not. / No, she isn't. She's **reading.**
	Are	you		Yes, we are.
				No, we're not. / No, we aren't. We're **swimming.**
		they		Yes, they are.
				No, they aren't. / No, they're not. They're **working.**

Spelling rules for verb + *ing*

In most cases, add *ing* to the base form of the verb: *work → work**ing***

If the verb ends in an *e*, drop the *e* and add *ing*: *exercis<u>e</u> → exercis**ing***

If the verb has one syllable and ends in a consonant + vowel + consonant, double the final consonant and add *ing*: *si<u>t</u> → sit**ting*** (This does not apply if the verb ends in *w, x,* or *y: ro<u>w</u> → row**ing**.)

A Complete the sentences with the appropriate words. Use contractions where possible.

1. A: _____*Are*_____ you (take) _____*taking*_____ the bus?

   B: No, _____. I (walk) _____.

2. A: What _____ they (do) _____ at the gym?

   B: They _____ (run) _____ and (swim) _____.

3. A: _____ you (use) _____ this computer?

   B: No, we _____. We (talk) _____.

4. A: Where _____ she (study) _____?

   B: At the English lab. She (listen) _____ to questions and (write) _____ the answers.

5. A: _____ he still (sleep) _____?

   B: No, he _____. He _____ already (work) _____.

LESSON B

The Present Continuous Tense: Extended Time	
A: What **are** you **doing** <u>right now</u>? B: I**'m studying** for a test <u>at the moment</u>.	You can use the present continuous to talk about actions happening now, at the moment of speaking. Notice the <u>time expressions</u>.
A: What **are** you **doing** <u>these days / nowadays</u>? B: I**'m studying** in Hong Kong <u>this term</u>. A: **Are** you **enjoying** Hong Kong? B: Yes, I**'m having** a great time!	You can also use the present continuous to talk about actions continuing for a period of time in the present. Notice the <u>time expressions</u>.

A Monika is traveling in Ecuador for a month. Read her email to a friend. Complete the sentences with the present continuous tense.

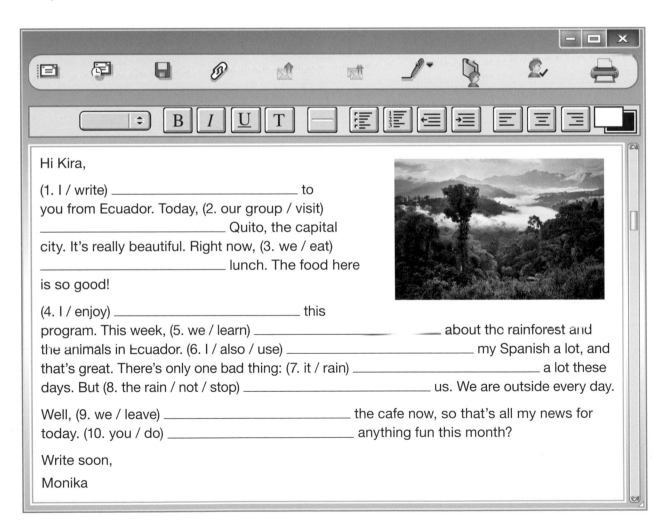

Hi Kira,

(1. I / write) _____ to you from Ecuador. Today, (2. our group / visit) _____ Quito, the capital city. It's really beautiful. Right now, (3. we / eat) _____ lunch. The food here is so good!

(4. I / enjoy) _____ this program. This week, (5. we / learn) _____ about the rainforest and the animals in Ecuador. (6. I / also / use) _____ my Spanish a lot, and that's great. There's only one bad thing: (7. it / rain) _____ a lot these days. But (8. the rain / not / stop) _____ us. We are outside every day.

Well, (9. we / leave) _____ the cafe now, so that's all my news for today. (10. you / do) _____ anything fun this month?

Write soon,

Monika

B Answer the questions. Write the numbers (1–10) from **A** on the correct line.

Which sentences in **A** are about…

1. actions happening right now? _____
2. actions continuing for a period of time in the present? _____

ADDITIONAL GRAMMAR NOTES

Possessive Nouns		
Singular nouns (+ 's)	**Plural nouns (+ ')**	**Irregular plural nouns (+ 's)**
sister → sister**'s** brother → brother**'s**	parents → parents**'** brothers → brothers**'**	children → children**'s** women → women**'s**

For first and last names that end in *s*, you can add **'s** or just **'**.

A Look up the word *twin* in a dictionary. Read about Hallie Parker and Annie James from the movie *The Parent Trap.* Complete the sentences with a singular noun, a plural noun, or a possessive noun.

1. Hallie Parker lives in her (father) _____ home in California, in the US.

2. Annie (James) _____ home is in London. She lives there with her (mother) _____.

3. The two (girl) _____, Hallie and Annie, are (twin) _____! But they live apart. They don't know about each other.

4. (Hallie) _____ summer plans are exciting. She's going to summer camp. And by chance, (Annie) _____ is going to the same summer camp!

5. At camp, Hallie sees her (sister) _____ face for the first time. They look the same! They are both surprised and happy.

6. Hallie doesn't know her (mom) _____ name, and Annie doesn't know her (dad) _____ name.

7. Before the two (child) _____ leave camp, they have an idea. The two (sister) _____ plan is an exciting one!

B What do you think happens next? Write three sentences. Tell your partner.

_____.

_____.

_____.

	Possessive Adjectives	Possessive Pronouns	*belong to*
Whose passport is this?	It's **my** passport. **your** **her** **his** **our** **their**	It's **mine.** **yours.** **hers.** **his.** **ours.** **theirs.**	It **belongs to me.** **you.** **her.** **him.** **us.** **them.**

Whose and *who's* have the same pronunciation but different meanings.
Whose asks about the owner of something: *Whose house is that? It's mine.*
Who's is a contraction of *Who* and *is*: *Who's studying English? Maria is.*

A Write the correct possessive pronoun for the underlined words.

1. A: That's not her suitcase.

   B: No, <u>her suitcase</u> is over there.

hers

2. A: Can I use your cell phone? <u>My cell phone</u> doesn't work.

   B: Sorry, but I forgot my cell phone at home. Use <u>Jon's phone</u>.

3. A: Is your class fun?

   B: Yes, but <u>Aya and Leo's class</u> is more interesting.

4. A: Is your hometown hot in the summer? <u>My hometown</u> is.

   B: <u>Our hometown</u> is, too.

5. A: Your birthday is in May.

   B: That's right, and <u>your birthday</u> is in March.

B 🔁 Use the words in the chart to complete the conversation. Then practice the dialog with a partner.

JIM: Well, I have (1.) _____*my*_____ luggage. Where's
(2.) _____ ?

BEN: Um... let's see... oh, here's (3.) _____
suitcase. No, wait... this one isn't (4.) _____ .

JIM: (5.) _____ is it?

BEN: It says Mr. Simon Konig. It belongs to
(6.) _____ .

JIM: Hey, I think that man has (7.) _____
suitcase. See? He probably thinks it's
(8.) _____ .

BEN: I'll ask him. Excuse me, does this suitcase
belong to (9.) _____ ?

SIMON: Oh, sorry. My mistake! I thought it was (10.) _____ !

Answers

Communication page 23

1. Brasilia **2.** Chinese **3.** FREE **4.** United Arab Emirates **5.** Cairo **6.** New York City **7.** FREE **8.** Russia **9.** Chile **10.** Answers will vary. **11.** FREE **12.** Jakarta **13.** The British Royal Family **14.** Germany **15.** Thai **16.** FREE **17.** Kuala Lumpur, Malaysia **18.** Venice **19.** English, French **20.** Austria **21.** Brazil, Colombia, Peru, Bolivia, Venezuela, Ecuador **22.** FREE **23.** Answers will vary.

NOTES

NOTES

NOTES

NOTES